This book belongs to

____

Things I Want To Say At Work But Can't

I DON'T
GET PAID
Enough
FOR THIS
Shit

I'M
CURRENTLY
WORKING TO
A Deadline,
IT'S CALLED
Fucking
FRIDAY

Great News
THE BOSS
JUST HIRED
ANOTHER
Fucking
Idiot

HOPE THIS
HELPS
=
LEAVE ME
THE FUCK
ALONE

LOOKS LIKE
IT'S
Fuck This
SHIT
O'clock

SORRY
IM LATE,
I HAD BETTER
SHIT
TO DO

THIS MEETING
COULD
HAVE BEEN
A FUCKING
EMAIL

FRIDAY
IS MY
SECOND
FAVOURITE
F WORD

I CAN'T WORK
Today
BECAUSE
I'M SICK
OF THAT
Fucking
PLACE

I'VE ALREADY GIVEN
100%
THIS WEEK
AND IT'S
ONLY
Fucking
MONDAY

HOW ABOUT
NEVER?
IS NEVER
FUCKING
GOOD FOR YOU?

SEE YOU
NEXT WEEK
FUCKFACE

WHO DIED
AND
MADE YOU
FUCKING
Boss

NO I CAN'T
WORK LATE
MOTHERFUCKER

SORRY
I'M REALLY
BUSY Today.
I'M COUNTING
DOWN THE Days
UNTIL MY
FUCKING
Retirement

SCREW YOU!

DON'T ASK ME TO DO A FUCKING THING UNTIL I'VE HAD Coffee

WARNING
PISSED OFF
APPROACH
WITH
CAUTION

I DON'T NEED TO CALM DOWN, I NEED PEOPLE TO STOP DOING STUPID SHIT!

SCREW THIS!
I'M GOING
HOME

MAYBE
SOMEONE
ELSE
COULD DO
SOME
FUCKING
WORK?

I CAN SEE YOUR
POINT,
BUT I STILL
THINK YOU'RE
AN
ASSHOLE

I KNOW I'M ALREADY HERE BUT IS IT TOO LATE TO CALL IN SICK

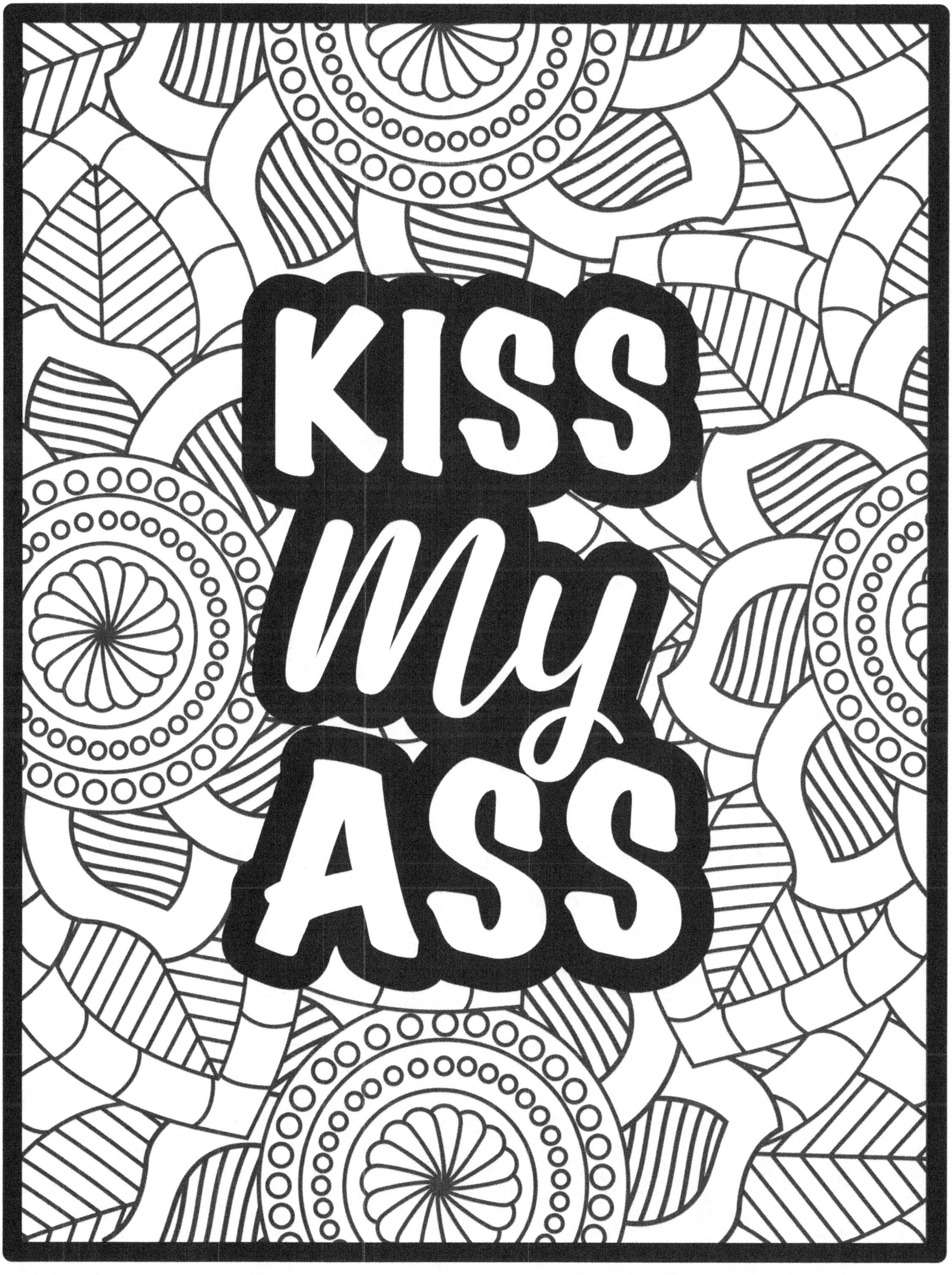
KISS
My
ASS

TELL
SOMEONE
WHO
GIVES A
CRAP

SORRY I CAN'T
WORK TODAY,
I FRACTURED
MY
FUCKING
MOTIVATION